D1517774

CROCKETT MEDIA CENTER

The Animal Kingdom

ANIMAL CAMOUFLAGE

Malcolm Penny

Illustrated by Carolyn Scrace

The Bookwright Press
New York · 1988

The Animal Kingdom

The cover shows some animals that blend in well with the lush South American rain forest. They are:

① Red-eyed tree frog   ⑤ Three-toed sloth
② Katydid   ⑥ Vine snake
③ Stick insect   ⑦ Draconian moth
④ Iguana

First published in the
United States in 1988 by
The Bookwright Press
387 Park Avenue South
New York, NY 10016

First published in 1987 by
Wayland (Publishers) Ltd
61 Western Road, Hove
East Sussex BN3 1JD, England

© Copyright 1987 Wayland (Publishers) Limited

ISBN 0–531–18166–9

Library of Congress Catalog Card Number: 87–71057

Typeset by DP Press, Sevenoaks, Kent, England
Printed by Casterman SA, Belgium

Contents

The art of camouflage

Camouflaged animals look like something they are not. Some look like part of a plant, some like another animal, and some like nothing on earth. Others have colors that blend in with the general background. For example, lizards that live in grassy places are usually green, while their relatives in deserts are sand-colored.

An animal that is regularly hunted has camouflage that makes it harder to find, while a hunting animal, or predator, has camouflage that hides it from its prey. Moths, which must rest during the day, provide some amazing examples of camouflage that protects them from being eaten by birds. Some moths look just like a leaf or the bark of a tree. Tigers are striped to blend in with shrubby

This thorny stem is really a cluster of insects called thorn bugs. By grouping themselves together, these insects create a wonderful disguise and so fool their predators.

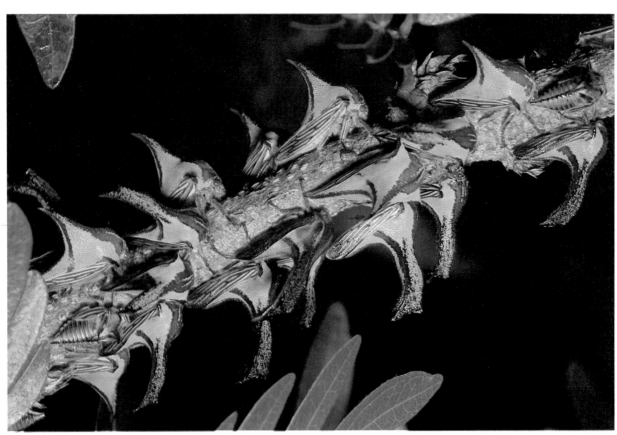

undergrowth. Because of their camouflage they do not frighten their prey away as they creep close enough to pounce.

Some animals are camouflaged by their shape, or by the way they move. There are spiders that look like ants, and a moth that flies like a bee.

Humans use camouflage, too. Green and brown battledress makes a soldier obvious in a street, but in a field or in the jungle it makes him harder to see. By sticking leaves into his helmet, the soldier blends in even better with the plants around him.

Even artificial structures are camouflaged so they will not show up. Ships in the Navy are painted gray, and some highway bridges are blue.

However, camouflage invented by humans is not nearly as effective as the disguises created by nature. In this book we shall look at some of the amazing disguises that creatures use to hide from their predators or prey.

The polar bear's white coat matches the snow, helping to hide the animal as it hunts seals.

5

Blending with the background

It often happens that an animal's color matches its background. Creatures of sandy deserts are usually sand-colored — snakes, desert foxes and gerbils, for example. Animals that live on black volcanic rocks are black to match the rock – marine iguanas of the Galapagos Islands are a good example. In snowy countries many animals are white, like the polar bear.

Some animals change color to match their surroundings. That well-known camouflage artist, the chameleon, and the sea-dwelling squid can change their color from one minute to the next. Other animals change color season by season. For example, Arctic hares and ptarmigan on the tundra turn white in winter to blend in with the snow. When spring comes the ptarmigan molts in patches, the new feathers being mottled brown.

Below left *The fennec fox and the four-toed jerboa blend with the sands of the Sahara Desert, where they live.*

Below right *Marine iguanas match the black volcanic rock of the Galapagos Islands, which lie west of Ecuador in the Pacific Ocean.*

This matches the patchy background as the snow melts, revealing clumps of moss and lichen. The Arctic hare also gradually turns brown as spring approaches.

Best of all, perhaps, at matching their background are the glass-winged butterflies of South America. Instead of changing their color to match their background, they have transparent wings and hardly show up at all.

Another way to disappear into the background is to be counter-shaded. This means that an animal's underside is paler than its back, making it harder to see because it looks less solid.

When artists want to make an object look solid, rather than flat, they paint the side that faces away from the light darker, because it is in shadow. Animals do the opposite, having their bellies paler than their backs, so that light from the sky makes them look the same color all over. They look flat, not solid, and merge in with the background.

Below left *In winter the snowy owl, ptarmigan and Arctic hare are white like the snow.*

Below right *During the spring thaw, the Arctic hare and ptarmigan molt to match the vegetation.*

Changing color

Chameleons are well known for being able to change color, but frogs, squid and some fish can also do so. They all do it in the same way, using color cells in their skin.

The color cells work in one of two ways. Those of chameleons and frogs have finger-like extensions all around the edge. The color can flow out to the ends of these extensions so that the cell shows up, or else it can be withdrawn into the middle, so that the cell becomes transparent (clear colored).

The range of colors in the cells is usually limited to the greens and browns of the forests or ponds where the animals live. There is a mountain chameleon in Africa that is an exception, having blue, black and yellow cells, as well as the usual range of colors.

Chameleons occasionally imitate something, instead of blending in with their background. One in Madagascar turns from pale brown to gold and dark brown when it is frightened, and drops motionless to the ground. Lying there, it looks exactly like a piece of dead wood, covered with mold, and it stays like that until the danger passes.

Squid have a different type of color cells. Theirs are bags of color, controlled by tiny muscles around the edge which can pull them out flat. With these cells, squid can change color very quickly, through a range from black, through pink and blue, to white. Sometimes the color ripples along the squid's body, imitating the light falling on it through the surface of the sea.

Opposite *The flap-necked chameleon,* Chamaeleo dilepsis, *can change its color to blend in with different backgrounds.*

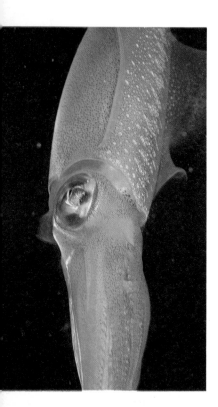

You can see the different colors in the body of this squid, which was photographed deep in the ocean.

Causing confusion

Another method of camouflage is to have a pattern that conceals the animal's true shape. Snakes that are boldly banded in contrasting colors, or covered with large blotches, conceal their long thin shape in this way.

A zebra's stripes make it very obvious in the zoo, but on the African plains, in a shimmering heat haze, they break up the outline of its body and make it harder to see. Another advantage is that the stripes enable an individual zebra to hide within a herd. A predator finds it hard to tell where one zebra ends and the next begins – their stripes merge together into one confusing pattern. The okapi and the bongo are two African antelopes whose velvety brown coats also are striped, to break up each animal's outline.

The Australian hairstreak, Thecla toyarna, *confuses its predators with a false head on its hind wings. The eyespots of the European peacock distract predators from attacking the butterfly's head or body.*

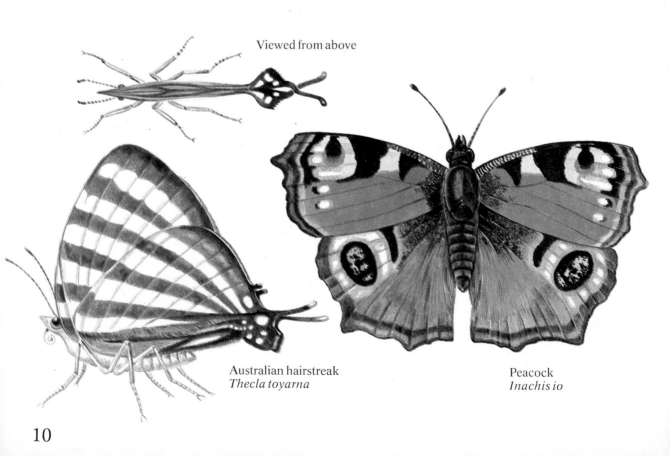

Viewed from above

Australian hairstreak
Thecla toyarna

Peacock
Inachis io

The badger, zebra and angel fish all conceal their eyes with a stripe.

The parts of an animal that give it away most readily are its round, dark eyes, so it is important to disguise them. Some animals and birds have pale-colored eyes that blend with their coloring. Many animals, from fish and birds to mammals, hide their eyes with a dark patch or stripe. Examples include butterfly and angel fish, pandas, zebras and badgers, and birds like avocets, nuthatches, cardinals and bee-eaters.

The eye is also a common place for a predator to attack. The European peacock butterfly has "eyes" on its wings, to draw attention away from its body. If a bird attacks the eyespot, the butterfly can still fly away, even with a piece missing from its wing.

The Australian hairstreak butterfly uses a very clever trick to fool its predators. On the rear edges of its hind wings, it has markings that look like a head, complete with waving antennae. If a bird decides to eat it, the butterfly has a fifty-fifty chance of escaping, depending on whether the false or real head is attacked.

11

Animals disguised as plants

Flower mantids of tropical Asia are masters of deception. Can you see where the flower ends and the insect begins?

Opposite *A scene from the South American rain forest, showing a number of camouflaged animals. A key is printed opposite the Contents page.*

Many animals that live among grass or leaves are green. Tree frogs and tree snakes of tropical rain forests are good examples of this, and so are many caterpillars and grass snakes. The sloth of the South American rain forest blends in with the vegetation because its shaggy, grayish coat is covered with green algae.

There are many creatures whose shape, as well as their coloring, camouflages them among plants. Leaf insects and stick insects are familiar examples. Other insects that look just like leaves are the katydids (or bush crickets) of North and South America. These small members of the grasshopper family have bodies shaped just like a fallen leaf, which may be bright green, yellow or brown.

Moths and caterpillars are well known for their ability to hide among plants and escape their predators. Some moths match the bark of a tree, others resemble dead leaves and others still look like a broken twig.

Some insects are colored and shaped to look like flowers. There are tropical mantids, whose bodies and legs perfectly resemble the petals of flowers, such as tropical orchids. Blossom spiders also imitate flowers to perfection. For example, the bell heather spider looks exactly like a purple heather flower. Both the flower mantid and the blossom spider use their camouflage to fool their prey. They wait on a flower and then seize an insect when it comes to gather nectar or pollen.

Some kinds of tree hoppers, which live in tropical countries, have bodies shaped like long, pointed thorns. When these insects, or "thorn bugs," are clustered together on a stem, they look just like a thorny stem and deter a predator from eating them.

Some clever illusions

There are some animals whose camouflage is most unexpected. Many small beetles, especially the round brown weevils that are found among nettles, "play dead" when they are disturbed. They fold their legs close to the body and drop to the ground, where they look exactly like grains of soil, fooling the birds, which otherwise would eat them.

Many of the lizards that live in deserts are spiny, partly to protect them from the heat, but also to make them unappetizing to predators.

Smooth lizards sometimes use an optical illusion to keep hawks from eating them. A pattern of dark and light bands on the lizard's back looks like the light reflecting off rows of spines. An example is the matuasto lizard, which lives in South America.

Concealed among the branches of this tree are two tawny frogmouths. Notice how their tails and the feathers on their faces resemble a splintered branch.

A similar trick is played by a small black and white sea slug. Its colors and pattern are almost the same as those of a hard, inedible black and white sea snail, which lives in the same parts of the seabed.

The tawny frogmouth of Australia is an extraordinary bird of the nightjar family. Its feathers perfectly match a tree branch, which is where the bird roosts motionless during the day.

In the previous chapter we have looked at insects that resemble plants. There are also flowers that look like insects, especially among the orchid family. An Australian slipper orchid looks and smells like a female wasp. Male wasps are attracted to the scent from over a mile away. When a male wasp tries to mate with the wasp-like flower, pollen grains become stuck to his abdomen. Soon he will try to mate with another flower and, in doing so, will transfer the pollen to it. Similar wasp, bee and fly orchids grow in Europe.

The markings of the matuasto lizard fool predators because the lizard appears to be spiny, although in reality it is smooth.

15

Dressing up

One way for an animal to be sure that it matches its background is to dress itself up in materials from its immediate surroundings. The decorator crab is a marvelous example, found around the coasts of Europe.

It is covered with sharp spines, which are used to hold in place pieces of seaweed that the crab breaks off from clumps nearby. The crab uses its claws to impale the weed on the spines. Because the pieces of weed are still alive, and continue to grow, they match perfectly the clumps of seaweed where the crab is hiding.

If the crab moves to another place where the weed is different, it removes its first disguise and replaces it with a new one, picked from the nearest clump.

*Illustrated **below** are four different species of caddis fly larvae, each protected in its camouflaged casing. Three of them have disguised themselves with shells, leaves or twigs. The fourth one has moved into an empty shell.*

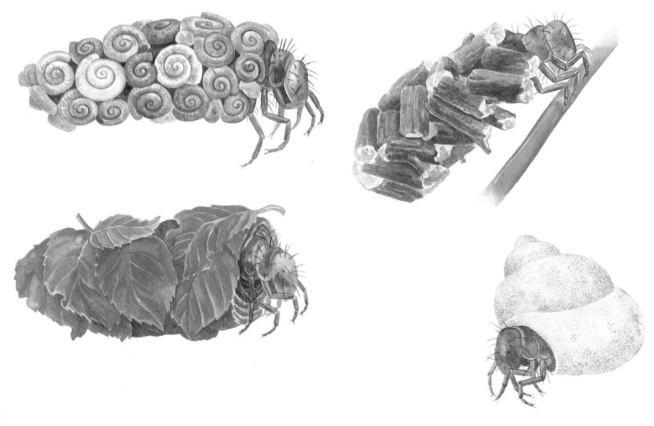

The sole's speckled body perfectly matches the sandy seabed but its fins are more noticeable, so the sole shakes a fine layer of sand over them to complete its disappearing act.

Caddis fly larvae of freshwater pools and streams and case moth caterpillars, which live in Australian woodlands, build themselves tubes to live in. Caddis fly larvae use a variety of materials to cover their tubes. They may use tiny pieces of gravel, snipped-off sections of water weed or empty shells. Case moth caterpillars make their cases from small pieces of twig or grass. Each species uses a different design.

The creatures mentioned above are perfectly camouflaged, because the materials that they use are part of their background. Other animals disguise their nests, rather than themselves.

Some hummingbirds use spiderweb to stick pieces of lichen to their nests, so that they blend with the branch where the nest is built. Tailor ants in Australia and harvest mice in Europe both make their nests out of living leaves or grass blades. Because the leaves are still alive, they remain the same color as the plants around them and so are well concealed.

Startling the enemy

A common way for small animals to escape being eaten is to startle the predator. Some do it by squealing or showing their teeth, but many, especially insects, do it by suddenly showing a patch of bright color. This is called "flash coloration."

Tiger moths are a good example. They have bright red hind wings that are hidden when the moth is at rest. If the moth is disturbed, it spreads its wings. The sudden flash of red startles the animal that was about to eat it, and gives the moth a moment to escape. African grasshoppers have red wings that produce the same effect.

Another way to make your enemy jump is to seem to turn into a much larger animal. An expert at this trick is the South American peacock moth.

The Virgin tiger moth of Canada and the United States flashes its red hind wings to scare off its enemies. The American swallowtail's caterpillar can make itself look like a large-eyed snake if it is threatened. This is shown in the inset circle.

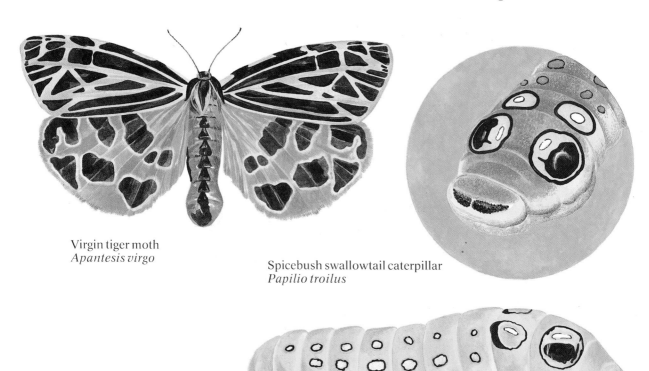

Virgin tiger moth
Apantesis virgo

Spicebush swallowtail caterpillar
Papilio troilus

Tiger Swallowtail caterpillar
Papilio glaucus

This creature has large, staring "eyes" on its hind wings, which are suddenly revealed when it is disturbed.

The caterpillar of the swallowtail butterfly of North America has eye markings near the front of its body. Normally they do not look very convincing because they are in the wrong place, but if a predator approaches, the caterpillar pulls in its head and hunches its body. Now the eyes are right at the front and the caterpillar looks like a snake.

The elephant hawk moth caterpillar uses the same technique. This trick would not work for a very small caterpillar – even if a bird thought it was a snake, it would happily eat it. So when they are small, elephant hawk moth caterpillars are leaf green, to be as inconspicuous as possible. They molt into their eye-marked skin when they are large enough for the disguise to be effective.

When alarmed, the caterpillar of the puss moth rears up one end of its body and draws in its head, revealing a bright red rim. It also lashes out with its two tail streamers. The South American peacock moth warns off its predators by suddenly revealing the large eyes on its hind wings.

South American peacock
Automeris memusae

Puss moth caterpillar
Cerura vinula

Looking poisonous

Poisonous animals, or those that taste bad, are often brightly colored. This reminds an enemy of the last time it tried to eat one, with unpleasant results. So when a predator sees the warning colors, it looks for something else to eat, and the poisonous animal goes free.

The warning colors are usually red, black and yellow, in various combinations. Snakes, frogs, fish, wasps, beetles, butterflies and caterpillars all use these colors to warn predators not to eat them.

Butterflies are a very good example of animals that advertise the fact that they are bad-tasting. In one family, which includes the monarch butterfly, the members have very similar patterns, even though they are different species. As a result, birds do not have to learn to avoid every species in turn. One unpleasant lesson teaches them to avoid the whole family.

The three butterflies **below** *use their red or yellow coloration to warn predators that they taste unpleasant. The very rare birdwing butterfly is from the Solomon Islands, the common rose from Sri Lanka and India, and the cinnabar moth from Europe.*

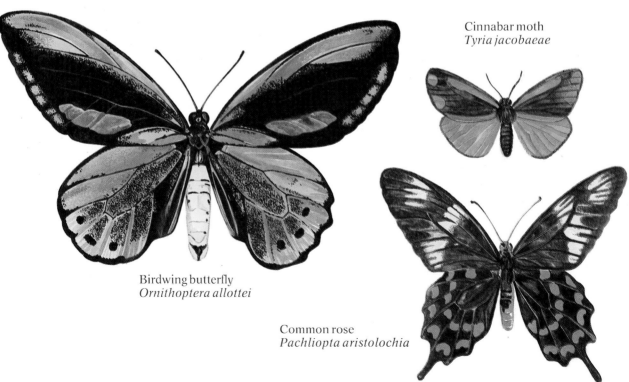

Cinnabar moth
Tyria jacobaeae

Birdwing butterfly
Ornithoptera allottei

Common rose
Pachliopta aristolochia

Above *The splashy yellow and black markings of this South American poison arrow frog clearly indicate to predators that it is poisonous.*

Below *The viceroy is an excellent mimic of the monarch butterfly.*

However, other butterflies from different families may imitate the monarch and its relatives. Unlike the butterflies they are imitating, they are not poisonous at all. However, because they look as if they might be, they, too, escape being eaten by birds. This imitation trick is called "mimicry."

Everyone who has ever been stung by a wasp, or even told about it by someone else, learns to avoid the black and yellow warning colors. So do birds. As a result, the garden in summer is full of black and yellow flying insects, which people avoid and birds will not eat. Most of them are not wasps at all, but flower flies, which are completely harmless.

Viceroy *Limenitis archippus*

Monarch *Danaus plexippus*

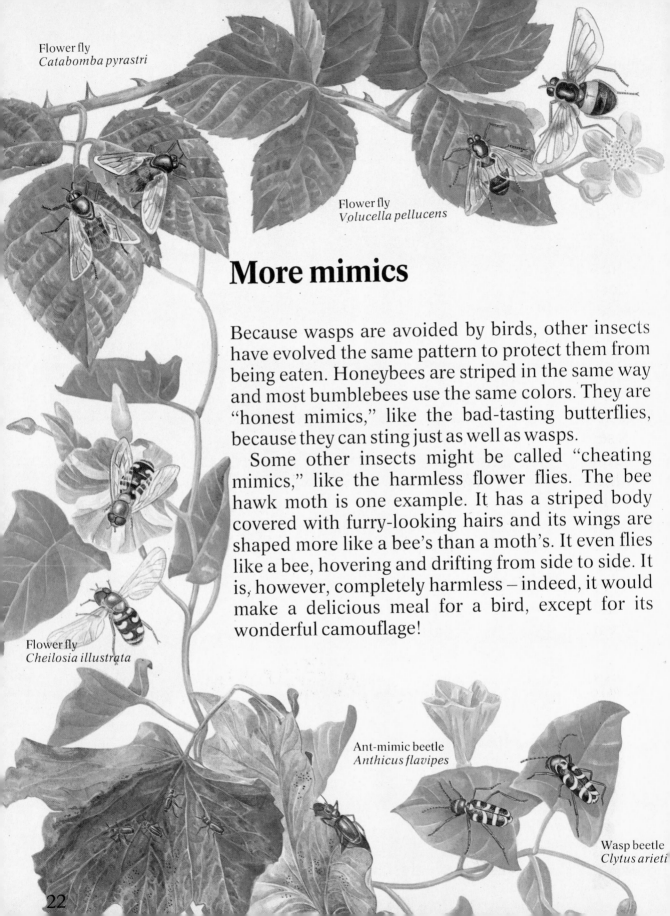

Flower fly
Catabomba pyrastri

Flower fly
Volucella pellucens

More mimics

Because wasps are avoided by birds, other insects have evolved the same pattern to protect them from being eaten. Honeybees are striped in the same way and most bumblebees use the same colors. They are "honest mimics," like the bad-tasting butterflies, because they can sting just as well as wasps.

Some other insects might be called "cheating mimics," like the harmless flower flies. The bee hawk moth is one example. It has a striped body covered with furry-looking hairs and its wings are shaped more like a bee's than a moth's. It even flies like a bee, hovering and drifting from side to side. It is, however, completely harmless – indeed, it would make a delicious meal for a bird, except for its wonderful camouflage!

Flower fly
Cheilosia illustrata

Ant-mimic beetle
Anthicus flavipes

Wasp beetle
Clytus arieti

The insects pictured here are all excellent mimics of other creatures.

Hornet moth
Sesia apiformis

The harmless wasp beetle pretends to be a wasp to protect itself from its enemies. It mimics a wasp, not only in its body markings, but in the way it carries its antennae, and the pattering way in which it walks.

The devil's coach horse is a large black beetle with short wing-cases, looking rather like a giant earwig. When it is alarmed, it curves its abdomen forward over its head, making it look very threatening. Of course, being a beetle, it too is harmless.

Some small black spiders mimic ants, moving around with them in and out of their nests. They walk in the same way, with quick, jerky movements and they are very hard to tell apart from the ants – their legs move too quickly to count! The spiders benefit from this in two ways: they can hide from their enemies by mingling with the swarm of ants; and they can occasionally eat a passing ant, which is unaware that its neighbor is a spider in disguise.

Narrow-bordered bee hawkmoth
Hemaris tityus

Devil's coach horse
Ocypus olens

Lobster moth larva
Stauropus fagi

Camouflage for attack

This photograph shows how well a lion blends in with the African savannah.

We have already met some animals that are camouflaged to help them to hunt, like the ant-mimic spider, or blotchy snakes such as pythons. There are many others.

The lion's light brown coat blends in perfectly with the dry grass of the African plains, where it hunts. Other hunting cats, like ocelots, leopards and cheetahs, have spotted coats that allow them to blend with the dappled dark and light background in woodlands. A tiger's camouflage is different – it has a striped coat because it commonly hunts in tall grass, where the shadows are vertical. Its bright golden background color makes it rather conspicuous by day, but in twilight or moonlight its camouflage is perfect.

The polar bear's permanent white coat conceals it in the snow. When it stalks seals, the bear creeps close to the ground and looks like a hummock in the snow. Inuit hunters also want to blend with the snow, so they carry a square wooden frame covered with white cloth in front of them when they stalk seals.

Two hunters that change their camouflage during the year are the Arctic fox and snowy owl. They are pure white during the Arctic winter, but when the snow melts, they molt into their brown spring coats.

The praying mantis has a leaf-shaped body, colored to match the leaves, among which it hunts smaller insects. However, the camouflaged mantis has an enemy, a slender green tree snake, which is also a master of disguise. The snake holds its body stiffly away from a branch, looking like a green twig with a bud on the end. If the snake can see the mantis, it has a good chance of catching it, because its own camouflage is so realistic.

Opposite *Lions and leopards are both well camouflaged, so that they can catch their prey, such as the young Thomson's gazelle shown here. An African rock python is hiding in the shade of the tree.*

Camouflaged eggs and babies

Birds that nest on the ground are in constant danger of having their eggs stolen by predators, so the eggs are often protected by camouflage. They usually have a pattern of irregular streaks and blotches, which serves two purposes. First, the pattern breaks up the outline of the egg's obvious shape. Second, it often makes the egg match the background on which it is lying. Some birds that nest on pebble beaches lay eggs that are very hard to tell apart from the stones around them.

When the eggs hatch, the young chicks are often gold and black colored to blend with the ground. If they sense danger, the chicks must lie quite still until the predator has gone away.

Cuckoos camouflage their eggs in order to trick another bird. They lay their eggs in the nests of other birds, which rear the cuckoo's chick as if it were their own. The cuckoo's egg must match the eggs of the other bird if it is to be accepted. So one kind of cuckoo lays blue eggs to match the eggs of the host bird, while another cuckoo lays speckled eggs to match the eggs of its host.

The eggs of the jacana, or lily-trotter, are patterned to match the dark waterweed that grows where the eggs are laid.

The young of many prey animals are often camouflaged as long as they are too small to run fast. A deer fawn has pale spots on its brown back, a pattern that helps to hide it among the clumps of dry bracken or small bushes where it is left by its mother. The spots look like sunlight falling through the leaves, making the fawn very easy to overlook, as long as it stays still.

A young topi antelope in Africa is sandy colored, to match the background of dry grass on the plains. When it grows older, it will take on the black markings of an adult. By then, it will be big enough to run from hunters, and to turn and fight if it is cornered by a predator.

Baby zebras stay very close to their mothers while they are small. Their striped coats merge together, making it very hard for a predator to see the foal beside its mother. Only the biggest hunters, such as lions, would attack an adult zebra, but many smaller ones will take a foal.

How did camouflage happen?

Cuckoo   Reed warbler

Cuckoo   Blue-headed

*The illustration **above** shows how well the eggs of the European cuckoo match those laid by other birds.*

Almost all animals use camouflage, either to escape predators or for help in catching prey. As we have seen, such animals are masters of the art of disguise.

The camouflage of all prey animals is kept perfect by their predators. An animal whose camouflage is not good enough will not live long – it will soon be seen by a predator. Only those with the best camouflage survive to produce young, and those young are likely to take after their parents and have good camouflage like them. This process is called natural selection. It works for the hunters as well – if their camouflage is not good enough, they will go hungry because their prey will see them a long way off and run away.

The camouflage of cuckoo's eggs mentioned in the last chapter is another example of natural selection. If the cuckoo's eggs do not match the host bird's eggs, they will be thrown out of the nest. So over thousands of years, their camouflage has evolved and become more realistic.

An extraordinary example of natural selection

The tiny South American lizard, Anolis capito, *is a master of camouflage. Its mottled colors blend in beautifully with fallen rain forest leaves.*

Opposite *The weedy sea dragon is a kind of sea horse found around the coasts of Australia. It looks so much like a clump of floating seaweed that small fish hide among the weed-like growth. Notice that the fish in the photograph has a false head to confuse its predators.*

evolved in Japan, hundreds of years ago, when the samurai crab was a popular food. The crab has a pattern on its back that looks more or less like the face of a warrior. Because warriors ruled Japan in those days, the fishermen thought it was very unlucky, even dangerous, to kill a crab with a warrior's picture on its back, so they threw the most realistic-looking ones back into the sea. The result is that all the samurai crabs today have extremely realistic faces on their backs. This, too, is natural selection, even though it was caused by human behavior.

Very few animals need no camouflage at all. Only animals that have no natural enemies, and whose food cannot escape, need not disguise themselves. On land, creatures without camouflage are the very big herbivores, such as elephants, rhinoceroses and hippopotamuses. In the sea, only huge creatures like humpbacked and right whales, which filter plankton for food, need no camouflage.

Glossary

Algae A group of simple green plants that grow in moist conditions.

Antennae The pair of "feelers" on the head of an insect or crustacean.

Battledress The mottled uniform worn by soldiers to help them blend in with bushes and hide from the enemy.

Evolved Developed over a long period of time.

Herbivores Animals that feed only on plants.

Impale To pierce an object with a sharp instrument.

Inconspicuous Hidden, barely noticeable.

Inedible Not good to eat.

Molt To shed feathers or fur.

Natural selection The process that results in the greatest number of young being produced by animals that are best adapted to their surroundings.

Predators Animals that prey on other animals.

Prey An animal that is eaten by another animal.

Tundra The vast treeless zone that lies between the frozen Arctic and the coniferous forests of North America and Eurasia.

Further information

If you would like to read more about camouflage, the following books are useful:

Animal and Plant Mimicry by Dorothy H. Patent. Holiday, 1978

Animal Disguises by Gwen Vevers. Merrimack Publishing Circle, 1982

Animals in Disguise by Peter Seymour. Macmillan, 1985

The Answer Book about Animals by Mary Elting. Putnam Publishing Group, 1984

Amazing Facts about Animals by Gyles Brandreth. Doubleday, 1981

Hidden Animals by Millicent Selsam. Harper & Row Junior Books

How to Hide a Polar Bear and Other Mammals by Ruth Heller. Putnam, 1985

Hunters and the Hunted: Surviving in the Animal World by Dorothy H. Patent. Holiday, 1981

When Winter Comes by Russell Freedman. Dutton, 1981

Wildlife on the Watch by Mary Adrian. Hastings, 1974

You can discover more about camouflage by watching for moths and caterpillars, and even amphibians or reptiles, in your yard or in the country. Zoos, and safari parks often keep leaf and stick insects and warning-colored snakes or frogs for visitors to look at. Some wildlife programs on television will also tell you more about camouflage.

You might like to join an organization that helps to protect wild animals and the habitats they live in. Some useful addresses are:

Audubon Naturalist Society of the Central Atlantic States
8940 Jones Mill Road
Chevy Chase, Maryland 20815
301–652–9188

The Conservation Foundation
1717 Massachusetts Avenue, N.W.
Washington D.C. 20036
202–797–4300

Greenpeace USA
1611 Connecticut Avenue, N.W.
Washington D.C. 20009
202–462–1177

National Wildlife Federation
1412 16th Street, N.W.
Washington D.C. 20036
202–797–6800

The Humane Society of the USA
2100 L Street, N.W.
Washington D.C. 20037
202–452–1100

The International Fund for Animal Welfare
P.O. Box 193
Yarmouth Port, Massachusetts 02675
617–362–4944

Picture acknowledgments

The publishers would like to thank the following for allowing their photographs to be reproduced in this book: Oxford Scientific Films 4 (Michael Fogden); Oxford Scientific Films/Mantis Wildlife Films 12, 28 (Jim Frazier); Seaphot/Planet Earth Pictures 8 (Bill Wood); Survival Anglia Limited 14 (Jen and Des Bartlett), 17 (Rod and Moira Borland), 21 (Mike Linley), 26 (Liz and Tony Bomford), 29 (Mike Linley). The photograph on page 24 belongs to the Wayland Picture Library.

Index